Old GOVANHILL

by

Eric Eunson

First Published in the United Kingdom, 1994
By Stenlake Publishing, Ochiltree Sawmill, The Lade, Ochiltree, Ayrshire KA18 2NX
Telephone/Fax: 01290 423114

ISBN 1-872074-49-9

This 1905 picture was taken behind the John Wesley Methodist Church, which stood at the corner of Cathcart Road and Butter-biggins Road. Built around 1870, it was the oldest church in Govanhill. In the 1980's the church was converted into a glazier's workshop, and the adjacent hall was made into flats. The former church was badly damaged by fire and later demolished in 1993.

INTRODUCTION

From ancient times until the middle of the 18th century the area occupied by Govanhill, Polmadie and Crosshill changed very little. It was composed largely of treeless heath and bog, intersected by sluggish, meandering streams and a few ancient tracks. The district lay on the much disputed boundary between the counties of Lanarkshire and Renfrewshire, and the parishes of Govan and Cathcart. Just how vague these boundaries were is illustrated in old deeds and charters which have Polmadie and Crosshill passing back and forth between counties and parishes at regular intervals!

The name Polmadie is often believed to derive its name from an incident during the retreat of Mary Queen of Scots from the Battle of Langside in 1568. Her exhausted steed, allegedly called "Poll", is said to have fallen and perished in the vicinity. It is a romantic and appealing tale, but completely apocryphal. Polmadie was already an old name by Mary's time and is first mentioned in the 12th century, when it was written as Polmacde. This has been interpreted as either "pool or stream in the field of God" or "pool of the wolves". The district was the site of the first hospital on the south of the Clyde. This was established by monks some time before 1249, to care for the poor of the city and surrounding districts. In 1320 Bishop John of Glasgow endowed the hospital with "the eastern part of Little Govan" (roughly the area of modern Polmadie), and the lands of Crosshill. In 1453 control of the hospital and its lands passed to the Church of Dumbarton, which continued to hold them until the Reformation in the mid-16th century. All record of the hospital disappears around this time, and its exact site is now unknown.

In the 17th century a small village existed at Polmadie, west of the boundary of Rutherglen which was marked by the Mall's Myre Burn. Among its inhabitants were Robert Thom and Thomas Cook, weavers, and John Urie who was a farm labourer. It was a period of religious turmoil in Scotland, and these three men signed their names to the Covenant, a document protesting against royal supremacy over the church. The covenanters were fiercely persecuted, and the three men appeared on a list of fugitives issued by royal proclamation in May 1684. On May 11th of the following year they were seized in their working clothes, blindfolded with scarves taken from passers-by, and shot without quarter. They were buried in a single grave in Cathcart churchyard, and a stone was later placed over it describing them as "three Uncommon men of Polmadie". This became known as the Martyrs' Grave, and a short service is still held annually at the graveside.

Old maps give the name of Crosshill as Coyshill or Corsehill. This name is supposed to derive from the ancient practice of marking the extremities of a parish with wooden crosses, usually made of elm. Crosshill lay on the northern edge of Cathcart parish, and the boundary is shown in the 18th century approximately following the line of Queen's Drive.

The political stability Scotland experienced during the 18th century provided opportunity for progress. One of the prerequisites for this was the improvement of the country's roads. At the beginning of the century the movement of goods by land was almost impossible. The existing tracks were nothing more than traditional footpaths, unmade and unmaintained, which followed the most direct or safest route from A to B. One such path followed part of present day Cathcart Road. In 1753 an Act of Parliament was passed to upgrade this track into "a road from Gorbals to Floak Bridge, by way of Corsehill and Cathcart, to the Kirk of Carmunnock". This road became a turnpike road, built and maintained by a private company who erected toll houses at various points along its length to pay for the upkeep of the road.

The late 18th century also saw a revolution in agriculture in Britain. Waterlogged land was drained to create fertile soil, open fields were enclosed by walls and hedges, implements were improved, and new crops introduced. During this period the area south of the Clyde changed dramatically. Prosperous new farms emerged on what had been uncultivated ground and the district began to be dotted with small country houses. There were two hamlets in the area of Govanhill. To the west of Cathcart Road lay Butterbiggins, and to the north-east was Little Govan, a collection of weavers' cottages and loomshops. In the 1840's the cottage industry of linen weaving was supplanted by factories, and plunged the handloom weavers into poverty. As a consequence Little Govan was abandoned and the owner of the village tore it down. The mansion of Little Govan was situated in what is now Oatlands, and a colliery of the same name stood where Cathcart Road is crossed by Allison Street. Around 1780 a young man named William Dixon became the manager and later lessee of this pit. In 1811 he built an ambitious waggonway from Little Govan to the canal basin at Port Eglinton. The mine was one of the most productive in Scotland. Dixon reinvested much of his profit from it in sinking other pits and developed the Calder and Wilsontown Iron Works. By the time he died in 1822 he was the foremost industrialist in Scotland. His son, also called William, was born in 1778 and inherited all of his father's business acumen. In 1839 he opened the Govan Iron Works at Gushetfaulds, at the top of Crown Street, and soon had five huge blast furnaces working. He also built the Govan Colliery School, the first in the area, for the children of his workers. William Dixon the second died in 1859, and the empire passed to his son William Smith Dixon. It was he who was responsible for the development of Govanhill.

William Smith Dixon bought the extensive estate of Little Govan in the 1860's, and began feuing the ground to builders in 1869, partly to provide housing for his workforce and also to cash in on the building boom that had gripped the city. Between 1872-6 the Dean of Guild Court (the equivalent of today's Planning Department) authorised the construction of more than 21,000 tenement houses around the city. Many of these were in previously undeveloped areas, and the suburbs of Springburn, Maryhill, Dalmarnock and Govanhill were largely laid out in this period. The Police Act of 1862 gave any settlement with a population exceeding 700 people the right to establish itself as a self regulating burgh, with the right to its own council, police force and fire service. Govanhill became an independent burgh of 7,212 inhabitants, on the 4th of July 1877. The public offices were located in Belleisle House, which still stands at the rear of Holy Cross Church on Dixon Avenue.

The development of neighbouring Crosshill began in the 1840's with some limited feuing of part of the policies of Crosshill House. It was one of several semi-rural suburbs of this type, built on the peripheries of Glasgow for the middle classes who sought to escape from the squalor and pollution of the overcrowded city centre. In 1870 the district consisted of three streets of large villas, and some high-class tenements on Langside Road, Victoria Road, and facing Queen's Park. Crosshill voted itself an independent burgh in a referendum in 1871.

Both burghs continued to grow steadily and by 1881 Govanhill had 9,636 inhabitants and Crosshill 2,960. Ten years later these had increased to 14,339 and 3,978 respectively. Between 1870 and 1891, 3,057 new houses were built in Govanhill. Glasgow was surrounded by these expanding burghs, and resented the independence of so many ratepayers who lay outwith the jurisdiction and coffers of George Square. Many bitter and protracted battles were fought with the Corporation, who claimed to have improved park, gas and water facilities in the suburbs. Finally, in 1891 Govanhill and Crosshill were annexed by the city, along with the burghs of Maryhill, Springburn, Hillhead, Mount Florida and East Pollokshields.

The original feuing restrictions placed on Govanhill stipulated that all houses had to have a minimum of two rooms, but some were inevitably sub-divided to form the notorious "single ends". In a survey of 1935 these were found to make up 2.8% of the area's housing, but this was still the sixth lowest statistic of any ward in Glasgow. The same survey revealed that 23.1% of Govanhill's population lived in 1,925 overcrowded houses, but again this figure is relatively low for tenement districts at that time.

When the sandstone tenements of Glasgow were erected, between 1870 and 1910, they were probably the best contemporary working class housing anywhere in Britain. In the mid 19th century the east end of the city contained some of the worst living conditions in Europe, and the City Improvement Trust was set up in 1866 to instigate a programme of slum clearance and controlled redevelopment. The strictness of the regulations laid down by the Trust and the Dean of Guild Court is illustrated by the fact that at the end of the century it cost 45% more to erect a four storey building in Glasgow than it did in London. Sadly, although the regulations governing building were stringent, rules about maintenance were not. Absentee landlords and their factors took a short term view of their property, and were only concerned with profit from rent. As a consequence, by the end of the Second World War many of the tenements were in a state of chronic disrepair. The post-war solution to the problem was "comprehensive redevelopment", and throughout the 1950's, '60's and '70's whole districts of the Victorian city were obliterated. On the south side, Kinning Park, Kingston, Govan, Pollokshaws, Dalmarnock and Gorbals were almost completely levelled, and in the early 1970's much of the eastern part of Govanhill followed suit. But public attitudes to tenements were changing. The high-rise flats and peripheral estates that were built to replace them had proved socially, and sometimes structurally, unacceptable and there was increasing pressure on the planners to repair rather than rebuild what remained of the tenements. The continued demolition of Govanhill was on the cards, and after 1970 a number of local residents groups were formed by people who wanted to save their homes. These gave rise to the formation of the Govanhill Housing Association in 1974. By 1992 more than 1,500 houses had been improved, at a cost of £31.5 million. In the mid 1970's the District Council implemented a scheme of grant aided stone cleaning. The first sand blasting methods used had been developed for stripping the barnacles off the hulls of tankers! Later chemical cleaners were used, but these too have become controversial. This was a cosmetic exercise, and it is still common to see a seemingly immaculate tenement having its guts torn out by the Housing Association, because the internal woodwork is riddled with dry rot. Govanhill remains the most intact of Glasgow's Victorian working class suburbs, and structurally at least its future seems secure.

Few Glaswegians called the Govan Iron Works by its "Sunday name", and to most it was known as "Dixon's Blazes". The flames from the blast furnaces lit up the night sky over the Gorbals and Govanhill for over a century. In 1849 one writer commented, "the bright glare cheers the long winter night, and at the same time does the work of a score of policemen, by scaring away the rogues and vagabonds who so plentifully infest other and darker parts of the city." For generations of south-side weans the Blazes were "the bad fire" where fractious children spent eternity. Hell was disconcertingly near to Govanhill! This postcard shows part of the works in 1905.

Govan Iron Works locomotive number 4 in 1948. The closure of the works in 1959 was a staggering blow to the surrounding community. The site was cleared during the early 1960's, the last remaining buildings were a brick engine house and adjoining offices facing Crown Street which dated from 1888. These were pulled down in 1968. The site is now occupied by an industrial estate and Castle Cash and Carry.

Alex Whyte was selling whisky for two and six and three bob, when this postcard of the corner of Aikenhead Road and Cathcart Road was published in 1907. Aikenhead Road follows the course of an old route to the mansion of Meikle Aikenhead. This was rebuilt in 1806 as Aikenhead House, which now stands in King's Park. These tenements were among the first to be erected in Govanhill around 1870, and were demolished a century later.

A 1908 photograph looking down Batson Street towards Aikenhead Road, from the corner of Jamieson Street. The tenement on the right has the openings for fireplaces and cupboards on the gable. Although streets of tenements present a uniform frontage they were usually built a few closes at a time by several different contractors. When this was the case, the gables were left in this way to facilitate the continuation of the block. All these buildings have now been demolished.

DUBS' WORKS, GLASGOW.

The Queen's Park Locomotive Works were opened in 1864. They were founded by the German engineer Henry Dubs, who had been a partner in William Neilson's loco works at Finnieston. Although his name was pronounced "doobs", the works were always known locally as "dubs" (as in puddle). By 1905 Dubs was the second largest builder of steam engines in the country, and employed 2,423 men. In the same year the factory merged with the Atlas and Hyde Park works in Springburn to form the North British Locomotive Company. The world trade slump of the 1920's and 1930's hit the company hard, although demand for engines recovered a little after World War Two. In 1948 the company began to make diesel and electric locomotives, but other firms had anticipated the change from steam power earlier and the North British began to lose orders. By 1956 the company was making huge losses. All three works closed in 1962 with a total loss of 5,000 jobs.

Polmadie was a mixed district of heavy industry and occasional blocks of tenements and this Edwardian postcard of Hamilton Street shows part of the Scotch and Irish Oxygen Company's Rosehill Works on the left.

The railway cutting through Polmadie was created in 1848 by the Caledonian Railway as part of their line from Carlisle to Glasgow and Edinburgh, via Carstairs. With the continued expansion of the rail network during the 1850's this railway became, and still is, the main route from the city to London. The engine shed on the left of this 1938 picture was built by the Caledonian in 1859.

These tenements on Cathcart Road (south of the junction at Aikenhead Road) were built on land that originally formed part of the grounds of Inglefield House. This house, which stood at the north of Butterbiggins Road, was demolished in the 1930's. Neighbouring Larkfield House only survived until the 1870's, and today the Larkfield bus depot occupies its site.

The same block is pictured here in 1907, looking north from the corner of Butterbiggins Road. These tenements were originally called Montgomery Place. Many blocks had extra names given to them by their builders which must have led to some confusion. The village of Butterbiggins stood between the road which took its name, and Govanhill Street. It was still standing in 1879 and maps show it consisted of seven substantial houses and two terraces. "Biggin" is a Scottish word for building, so Butterbiggins may once have been the home of a dairy.

The vista down Cathcart Road from Preston Street is still recognisable from this 1912 view, but the blocks on the right were pulled down in the early 1970's. The tram is bound for the terminus at Mount Florida, which remained the city boundary until the annexation of Cathcart in 1912.

The pink sandstone "Diamond Jubilee Buildings" were erected in 1897 by the Kinning Park Co-operative Society. They were refurbished by the Housing Association in 1991, but at the time of writing the retail units on the ground floor have still not all been let. Cathcart Road was once one of the busiest streets in the area, but now more than a quarter of its shops lie empty.

Contrasting types of tenements photographed around 1915. The left hand close is number 21 Smith Street (now Inglefield Street) and is typical of the buildings put up between 1870 and 1890. The facing of smooth sandstone blocks is known as ashlar. Tenements of this period used local blonde sandstone, mostly from the Giffnock Quarries. Note the caricatures of the Kaiser chalked on the extreme right of the wall. The right hand illustration shows a pink sandstone building containing numbers 115-7 Batson Street. Glasgow's quarries had become almost exhausted by 1895, and most buildings in the city built after this date used the pink stone which had to be imported from quarries at Lockerbie and Ballochmyle. Although bay windows became fashionable in middle class houses in the 1840's, they are seldom found in working class tenements before 1890, but were universal after 1895.

16

An atmospheric photograph of Preston Street, looking east from Cathcart Road, dating from 1912. This street, and its steep neighbours Jamieson, Carfin and Govanhill Streets were built on an area called Victoria Gardens in the 1870's. They were demolished almost exactly a century later and the site remained derelict for several years before the new houses were built.

More than forty children pose for the photographer in this 1903 picture of Govanhill Street, from the corner of Inglefield Street. The foreground remains almost unchanged but all the buildings beyond Cathcart Road have gone. New buildings on the site were completed in 1992.

VICTORIA PUBLIC SCHOOL

Parish School Boards were set up under the Education Act of 1872, which made it compulsory for every child to attend school from the ages of 5 to 13. Govanhill lay within the jurisdiction of the Govan Parish School Board which eventually built four schools to serve the area. These were Calder Street (1874), Annette Street (1886), Victoria Public School in Govanhill Street (1903), and Batson Street (1914). Govan School Board was considered the most progressive in Scotland and pioneered medical inspections, swimming baths and education for the handicapped.

New Band Stand, Govanhill Park.

In order to prevent the area becoming completely built up, Glasgow Corporation bought four acres of ground in 1894, to be laid out as a public park. The land consisted of prime building plots, and cost £3,000 per acre. The bandstand was added in 1903.

GOVANHILL PARK. GLASGOW.

A charming 1910 view with Coplaw Street to the left. Today this park is used mainly for "exercising" dogs. The children's swings have been replaced by an ash pitch and the bandstand is covered in graffiti; some of the trees are dying, and the turf which has replaced the flower beds is patchy. The tenements surrounding the park have been attractively refurbished but this little park remains sadly neglected.

This 1907 view of Govanhill Park is the work of W. Ross, who had a studio at 24 Paterson Street, Tradeston. Ross specialised in short runs of picture postcards of the suburbs of the city, and appears to have photographed every block in Govanhill! His photographs are of a high quality, and keenly sought by collectors today.

Col Mure

of Caldwell

Bo.t of Austin & Mc Aslan,

Nursery & Seedsmen.

Half Price Allowed for
returned Sacks & Packages
ONLY IF ADVISED.

Seed Shop, 16, Buchanan St. Nurseries, Coplaw Hill & Titwood.

1870						
Deer	21	10,000	Stg Scotch Fir		8	15
1871		2,000	— Thorn	x	2	.
Jany	17	3,000	Second Size Thorn	x	2	5
		1,000	extra fine Birch		2	.
		1,000	Alder			15
		1,000	Norway Spruce			14

The Austin & McAslan tree nursery at Coplaw Hill occupied the whole of the area now bounded by Victoria Road, Butterbiggins Road, Langside Road and Allison Street. By 1877 the firm had transferred all their growing to the Titwood Nursery, which lay in the Glencairn Drive area of Pollokshields. The Coplaw Hill site then became a brickworks to supply the frenzy of construction going on around it.

MILITARY FUNERAL AT GOVANHILL.
(The late Private JOSEPH PARVIN "90TH.")

The funeral of Joseph Parvin approaching the N.W. corner of Calder Street, circa 1908. Calder Street was partly laid out in the late 1870's, but ran only to the corner of Langside Road. Its full length was completed around 1900. Only the corner building and first close have survived from this view, the remainder have gone to make way for the Govanhill Health Centre of 1983.

The photographer chose typical Glasgow weather to capture John Webster's shop at the corner of Calder Street and Langside Road, in 1909. The advertising signs would now be valuable collectors items. This shop still trades as a grocer's today.

Govanhill Library was built on Coplaw Hill. It was designed by the architect James Rhind in Baroque style, and was opened in 1906. The statues symbolise learning. Externally the building remains almost unaltered.

Large Pond, Govanhill Baths, Glasgow.

The first baths in Govanhill were located in Butterbiggins Road where the filling station now stands. They were privately operated Turkish and Roman Baths, which opened in 1877. The Public Baths in Calder Street were designed by A.B. McDonald and opened in 1917. They consisted of hot baths in the upper storey, with three swimming pools on the ground floor. The "steamie" at the rear was converted into a launderette in 1971.

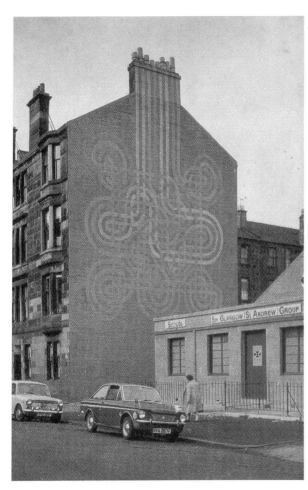

Left: In 1974 the Scottish Arts Council sponsored a pilot scheme of four gable end murals in tenement districts. The second, "Celtic Knot" by Jim Torrance, was completed in February 1975 on the gable of 30 Annandale Street. This was the first close refurbished by the Govanhill Housing Association in December 1975. Sadly the mural was destroyed during subsequent stone cleaning. The scout hut next door was demolished and rebuilt about five years ago.

Right: By the 1920's there were four cinemas in Govanhill proper. The Majestic in Inglefield Street (now the site of the Catholic Church); The Hampden Picture House in Westmoreland Street (now the Cladda Social Club), The Calder in Calder Street (demolished in the 1970's), and the Govanhill Picture House in Bankhall Street. The last of these is tucked away in a side street, and many locals are unaware of its existence although it is one of the most attractive buildings in the neighbourhood. It was designed by Eric Sutherland in 1926, with a tiled frontage of Egyptian columns, capped with bronzed Hindu domes. It closed as a cinema in 1961, becoming the inevitable Bingo Hall. It was later Greenlees Shoe Factory before conversion into a fabric warehouse.

No-one I have spoken to can remember the junction of Bankhall Street and Cathcart Road being called King's Cross, so it is possible the publisher of this 1907 postcard has made a mistake in his caption. In order to encourage his workforce in the habit of temperance, William Smith Dixon made it a condition of the feuing of Govanhill that there were to be no public houses in the burgh. It was a pretty hollow gesture, since there were five in Polmadie and any number of wine and spirit merchants in the area, but Govanhill remained dry for nearly a century. In 1962 the Penny Farthing, on the corner of Bankhall Street, became the first pub in the ward.

CATHCART·Rᵈ·FROM·ALLISON·Sᵗ·(2A)

Car number 381 heads towards Springburn in this otherwise traffic-free 1907 scene. As any local knows, this is now one of the most congested intersections in Govanhill. The tenements on the right were built in the 1890s on the site of the Little Govan Colliery. The architect of this block has included an attractive feature of Greek key pattern and rosettes below the second floor windows. Beyond can be seen the spire of the former Candlish Polmadie Church of Scotland. It was designed between 1874-7 by John Honeyman in a Gothic style. This prominent landmark has stood empty for many years and faces an increasingly doubtful future.

Govanhill Established Church was built around 1890 on ground that had also been occupied by part of the Govan Colliery. It was closed to worshippers in 1952 following a merger of congregations and stood empty for over twenty years before being knocked down. There is now a children's nursery on the site. The block on the left was formerly Ballochmyle Terrace, and was built along with the adjoining part of Daisy Street in 1893-4.

31

No. 3.

ALLISON ST

Allison Street, seen here from the corner of Langside Road in the mid 1900's follows part of the route of an old thoroughfare from Paisley to Rutherglen and Hamilton, which is believed to have existed in the 16th century. Like most of the streets in the area it was built over several decades by a number of different contractors. Different phases of development could merge to create an impression of continuity – the corner block in the foreground was built around 1865, but its immediate neighbours did not follow until the late 1870's. The block between Garturk Street and Daisy Street was put up in 1875 according to plans prepared by Alexander "Greek" Thomson, Glasgow's most famous Victorian architect.

This photograph was taken on the same day as the facing illustration and was obviously quite impromptu, as one of the shop staff was still straightening his tie when the shutter clicked. Today this shop is a branch of the ubiquitous Azad Video chain. There are three signs on the corner of the street – two reading Langside Road and one for Hope Terrace. The block on the north side of the street, between Westmoreland Street and Langside Road was formerly called Allanton Terrace, and took its name from an 18th century farm steading that once stood on the opposite side of the street.

CATHCART ROAD FROM DIXON HALL, CROSSHILL, GLASGOW.

In 1879 William Smith Dixon gifted a joint burgh hall to Govanhill and Crosshill which was, predictably, named after him. It was designed by Frank Stirrat in a style lying somewhere between Scottish Baronial and Victorian municipal Gothic. Dixon sought to encourage a spirit of co-operation between the burghs and the hall was built on the boundary, with two entrances, one on either side of the division. It is shown here around 1910. Since 1978 the Dixon Hall has been used as a day centre for the elderly.

34

HOLY CROSS CH. GLASGOW.

Belleisle Street takes its name from Dixon's country seat, Belleisle House near Ayr. This mansion is now a golf club-house. Holy Cross Church and its adjacent presbytery were designed in 1909-11 by Pugin and Pugin, the firm of architects responsible for scores of Roman Catholic Churches.

RELIABLE SERIES.

This postcard of Crosshill Boating Pond dates from 1907. The pond was situated on what is now a part of the playing fields of Holyrood School, and was filled in when the school was erected in the 1920's. At the turn of the century most of the ground to the east of Crosshill was still vacant land, and the pond was in an area known as Bawn Park. Beyond, towards Rutherglen, lay Mall's Myre, an expanse of marsh bisected by a burn of the same name, which flowed to the Clyde via Polmadie and Oatlands. Most of the burn was piped underground when the Toryglen housing scheme was built after the war, but the last part of it still survives as Jenny's Burn which flows through Richmond Park.

Dixon Road, Govanhill, Glasgow. S. 2

Govanhill was never a posh district, but neither was it an undesirable one. It was an area aspired to by the poor of overcrowded slum districts like Anderston, Calton and parts of the Gorbals. Council houses such as these in Dixon Avenue were erected after the First World War as part of Lloyd George's programme of building "homes fit for heroes". The 1919 Scottish Housing Act made provision for the erection of new houses, to be jointly financed by central government and local rates, and housing in the area was of a generally high standard.

Crosshill was robbed of its rural status by the expansion of Govanhill, and the remaining feus in the former burgh were built up with pink sandstone tenements around 1900. Crosshill Station opened in 1886 as part of the Cathcart District Railway. The station offices on the left were built at street level as there was no room for them on the narrow platform. They were demolished in the late 1950's when a small booking office was converted from part of the passenger shelter. The line was electrified in 1962.

WOUNDED ENTERTAINED BY QUEEN'S PARK, BOWLING CLUB. 21.9.16.

The inaugural meeting of Queen's Park Bowling Club was held on November 22nd 1866. At this meeting, a plot of ground facing Royal Crescent was chosen as the site for the greens. The ground belonged to the Corporation, and they stipulated that the greens should be laid out by Mr. McLellan, Parks Superintendent "in order that the amenity of the district should be strictly preserved"! The first clubhouse, an octagonal building of red brick, was erected in 1867, and two greens were formally opened for play on 13th June of that year.

In 1889 the club decided to add tennis courts to its attractions, and additional ground was leased from the corporation in 1889. By the end the year six courts had been constructed. In 1897 the club held "The Great Queen's Park Tournament" to raise funds to construct a third green. It was one of the largest and most successful bowling competitions ever held in Scotland, and attracted 788 entrants from all over the country. This superb wide angle photograph dates from around 1900 and shows the West Green. The conservatory on the left was built in 1889, and here members could sip tea amidst exotic plants and palm trees.

The old clubhouse was replaced by a larger one in 1929, while in 1938 it was decided that the conservatory had become unsafe, and it was taken down. The site was later used to extend the clubhouse. The popularity of bowling is reflected in the proliferation of clubs in the vicinity. In 1945 there were 33 private greens, 11 public greens and one indoor green, within a one and a quarter mile radius of Queens Park. D.L. Mackintosh, author of a history of the club wrote "One can make bold to say there is no other area of this size in the world which contains so many bowling greens." The dear "green" place indeed!

BALMORAL CRESCENT, GLASGOW

4040/62

The architect W.M. Whyte was responsible for this little bit of Paris in Crosshill, built between 1884-86. It created quite a stir in the burgh's Dean of Guild Court as it was alleged the original plans had been altered without their consent. This alteration included the inclusion of effigies of the builder and architect amongst the sculptures on the facade. By the early 1980's this elegant row was in a sorry state, with one building completely gutted by fire during its use as a hotel. However, painstaking restoration work carried out over several years was recently completed.

42

Royal Crescent, Crosshill, Glasgow

76422. JV.

Only the trees and tranquility of this street have changed. Royal Crescent was completed in 1870, while Campbell Douglas' Queens Park Church (visible in the background) was built between 1872-3.

In 1857 the Corporation bought Pathhead Farm from Neale Thomson of Camphill House, to create a new park to the south of the city. It was to be called Queen's Park, and plans for it were prepared by Joseph Paxton, the designer of the Crystal Palace. These proved too ambitious and were revised by the city's Master of Works, John Carrick. Although the location of the park was criticised at the time for being too far from the centres of population, it quickly provided the impetus for development of the surrounding area.

VICTORIA ROAD, GLASGOW.

A4936

In 1949 Glasgow experimented with the introduction of trolley buses on several routes in the city, including Cathcart Road and Victoria Road. These resembled conventional buses, but were powered by electricity from overhead wires, like trams. They were environmentally friendly, and had much smoother acceleration than diesel engined buses. They were also very quiet, which earned them the nickname "silent death" because you couldn't hear them coming! Despite all the advantages of the trolleys, noisy, jolting, fume-belching, diesel buses were cheaper to operate.

Victoria Road, Crosshill, Glasgow

47752JV

In 1880 Victoria Road still remained unbuilt north of Allison Street, and twenty years later did not extend beyond Calder Street. Although the view from the corner of Dixon Avenue has changed little from this 1907 scene, it does show the elegant period shopfronts, which have now given way to more modern facades.

46

This block at the corner of Allison Street was built around 1890, on the approximate site of the source of the Blind Burn. This burn led a winding course to the Clyde, and crossed Cathcart Road near Dixon's Blazes, until it was completely filled in during the 19th century.

This is the staff of the American Roller Skating Rink which was on Victoria Road, just opposite where Gateway Supermarket now stands. Roller skating was a craze which swept the country in the mid-1900's, and several rinks were opened in Glasgow. Evidently, our Edwardian forebears were as fickle as later generations, because the popularity of the pastime was short lived and most had closed by 1914.

Victoria Road showing B. B. Cinerama.

The roller skating rink was converted into the "B.B. Cinerama", although the cinema only occupied the building for a few years. In 1919 the B.B. moved to new custom build premises at the corner of Victoria Road and Butterbiggins Road. The former rink was removed in the early 1920's when the council built houses on the site. With a seating capacity of 2,700 the new picture house was the largest in the area, and also one of the longest running in Glasgow. Renamed the Odeon in 1964, it remained open until 1981. It was demolished soon after, and the site is now occupied by a filling station.

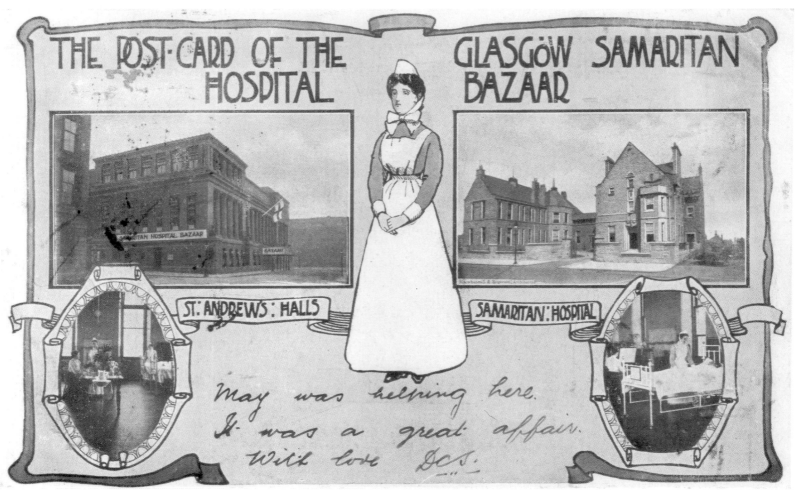

THE POST-CARD OF THE GLASGOW SAMARITAN HOSPITAL BAZAAR

ST. ANDREW'S HALLS

SAMARITAN HOSPITAL

May was helping here. It was a great affair. With love Dcs.

This postcard commemorates a 1903 bazaar that raised over £23,000 for the building of the Samaritan Hospital at Coplaw Hill. The original Samaritan Hospital, founded in 1886, had rented premises over a row of shops in Cumberland Street and only had three beds. The opening of a new, purpose-built hospital in the 1900's only came after a number of other previous moves and expansions. Annie French, one of the "Glasgow Girls" group of artists, designed the programme cover for the bazaar, and may also have designed this card.

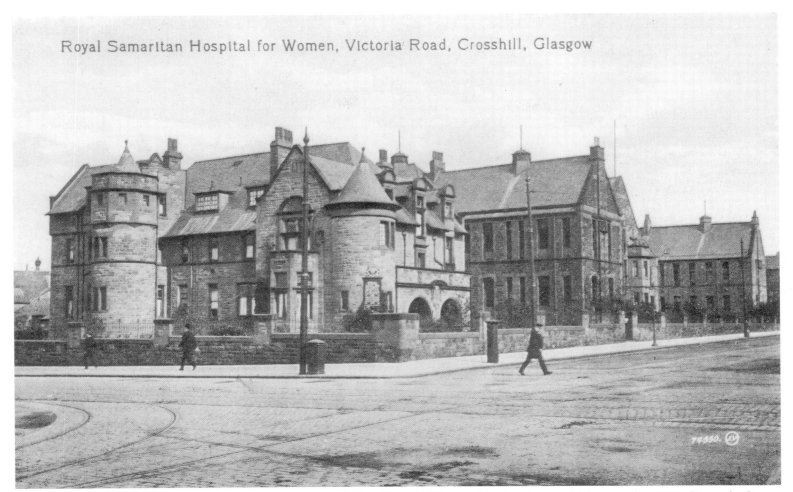

The building in the foreground of this view is the Alice Mary Corbett Memorial Nurses home which opened in 1906. It was built with money donated by a Mrs Polson as a memorial to her daughter who died in 1902. The funds from the bazaar were used to erect a new wing in 1907, which raised the capacity of the hospital to 83 beds. In the same year King Edward VII gave his approval to incorporate the word "Royal" in the name of the hospital.

SAMARITAN HOSPITAL, CROSSHILL, GLASGOW. B.4667.

The Samaritans held another fund raising bazaar in the St. Andrews Halls in 1924. This raised over £78,000 and completely paid for the addition of a further wing, completed in 1927. Between 1982 and 1986 the number of beds in the hospital was slashed, from 183 to just 79 and plans were put forward for its amalgamation with the Victoria Infirmary. Sadly, at the time of writing the Samaritan has recently closed and the buildings are for sale.